***Pan*-demonium** is a project devised and curated by Gillian Whiteley.
www.bricolagekitchen.com

This book is published in conjunction with the exhibition
***Pan*-demonium** presented at AC Institute [Direct, Chapel] 547 W 27th St, New York City, NY 10001, 3 September – 10 October 2009 www.artcurrents.org

Contents

bricolagekitchen on *Pan*-demonium

> In the street there was such merriment, noise and shouting...Some were amusing themselves with walking on their hands with their feet in the air, others were trundling hoops, or strutting about dressed as generals...Some were laughing, some shouting, some were calling out; others clapped their hands or whistled, or clucked like a hen that has just laid an egg. To sum it all up, it was such a pandemonium, such a bedlam, such an uproar....[1]

In 'Reflections on History and Play', Giorgio Agamben considers this famous scene in Collodi's novel when Pinocchio, who has travelled through the night on the back of a talking donkey, arrives in the 'infantile utopian republic' of 'Playland'. Agamben notes that such uproar not only destabilises everyday life and disrupts work patterns but it effectively destroys the calendar. Released from the burden of time,

---

[1] Agamben quoting C. Collodi *The Adventures of Pinocchio* (trans M.A. Murray) London: T. Fisher Unwin, 1892, in 'Reflections on History and Play' in Giorgio Agamben, *Infancy and History*, London: Verso. p. 75

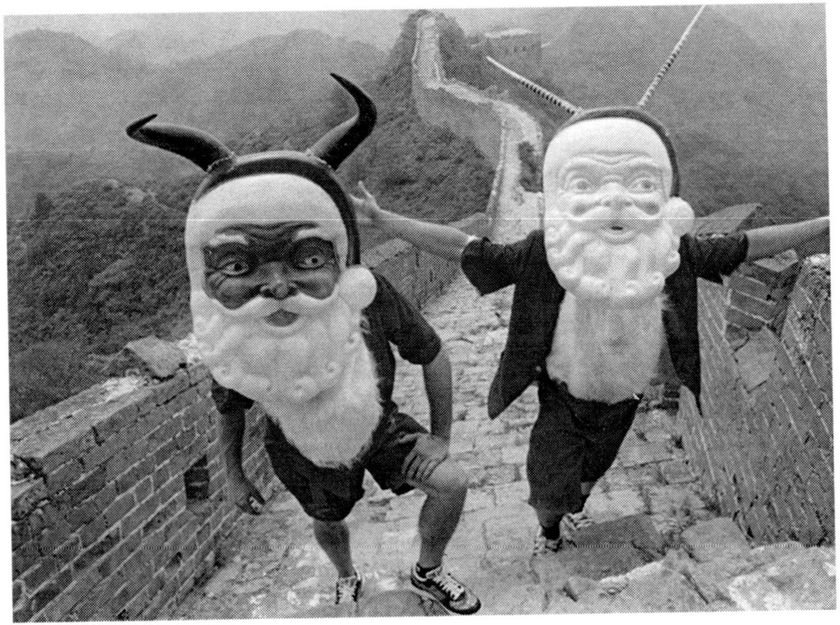

Andrew Erdos
Santalope, You Can't Keep us Out! 2008
Great Wall of China
Photo: Julianne Zimmerman

in Playland inhabitants enter another dimension of time: evidently, pandemonium can be a place of ecstasy and bliss. [2]

But pandemonium also has its dark side. The term—etymologically rooted in the Greek *pan* meaning all and *daemon*, Latin for spirit/demon—was also the name of Milton's capital of Hell in *Paradise Lost*. Along with nineteenth—century associations of lawless confusion and scenes of disorder, pandemonium is subject to negative readings with connotations of chaos and madness.

Recent history has witnessed much pandemonium. Walter Benjamin's rumination on Paul Klee's *Angelus Novus,* written in Spring 1940, anticipating the impending chaos of genocide and total war, reflects one such moment.

> A Klee painting named 'Angelus Novus' shows an angel looking as though he is about to move away from something he is fixedly contemplating. His eyes are staring, his mouth is

[2] Ibid p. 78

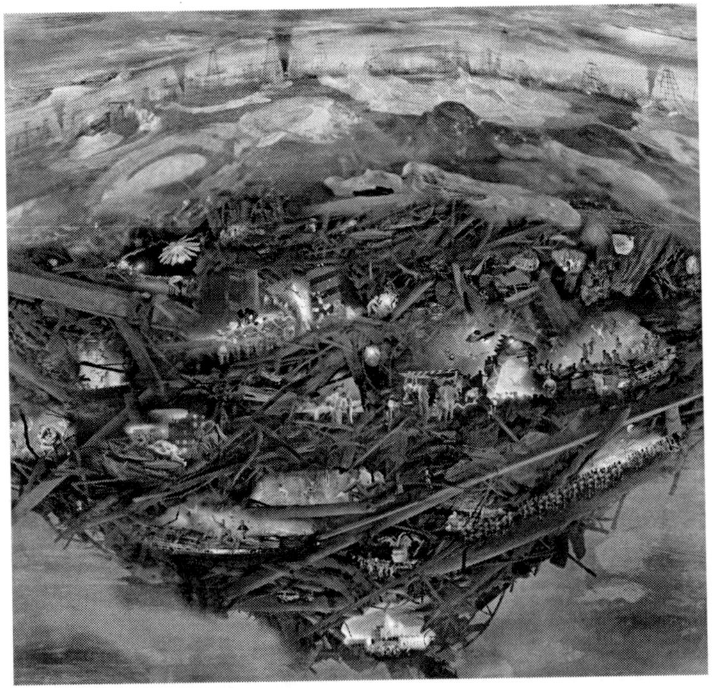

Paolo Consorti,
Hell 2009
Lambda print

> open, his wings are spread. This is how one pictures the angel of history. His face is turned toward the past. Where we perceive a chain of events, he sees one single catastrophe which keeps piling wreckage and hurls it in front of his feet. The angel would like to stay, awaken the dead, and make whole what has been smashed. But a storm is blowing in from Paradise; it has got caught in his wings with such violence that the angel can no longer close them. This storm irresistibly propels him into the future to which his back is turned, while the pile of debris before him grows skyward. This storm is what we call progress. [3]

Since Benjamin's apocalyptic vision, modernism has collapsed and the discourse of progress floundered. For Jacques Rancière, modernity—the Messianic culmination of Enlightenment rationality with its belief in science, progress and knowledge—has been undone.

---

[3] From 'Theses on the Philosophy of History' [1940] in Walter Benjamin, *Illuminations*, London: Pimlico, 1999, p. 249. Benjamin owned Paul Klee's small watercolour painting, *Angelus Novus* (1920).

> Postmodernism thus became the grand threnody of the unrepresentable/intractable/irredeemable, denouncing the modern madness of the idea of a **self-emancipation of mankind's humanity** and its inevitable and interminable culmination in the death camps....[4]

The final 'madness' of modernity has, arguably, been revealed and a series of 'ends' have accompanied postmodern thinking. Now, in a global era described by some as 'post-politics', any consensual notion of progress is naïve and yet, Benjamin's *Angelus* remains not only a powerful signifier of 'witness' but also a motif of hope in a crazy world. [5]

---

[4] Jacques Rancière, 'Artistic Regimes and the Shortcomings of the Notion of Modernity' in *The Politics of Aesthetics*, 2000 p. 29

[5] See Martin Archer/Geoff Bright, *Angelus Novus 1-5*, 2009, electro-acoustic audio which explores Scholem's poem and Benjamin's Ninth Thesis. Benjamin's allegorical use of Klee's 'angel' has been revisited extensively by artists, musicians (eg Laurie Anderson, John Zorn) and writers (eg Esther Leslie, *Walter Benjamin*, London: Pluto Press, 2000) Also, see the recent exhibition *Lost Paradise – The Angel's Gaze*, 2008 at www.paulkleezentrum.ch

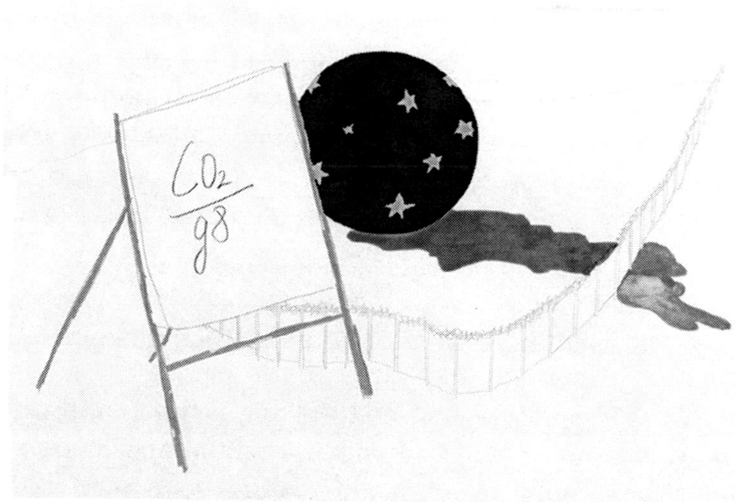

Stephan Weitzel
G8-Heiligendamm
2007
Drawing, mixed
media on paper

In contemporary terms, pandemonium seems to resonate with the current global political, ecological and economic situation—one in which the hegemonic forces of order have been overwhelmed by a dynamic of chaos and disorder, turning the world 'upside-down'. Indeed, this current 'crisis' may be a unique moment of pandemonium with its own particularities. However, it is also a *return*. For, as with the Deleuzian conception of the 'eternal return' [6], the topsy-turvy state of things represents the return of *difference* and this chaotic moment, as every other, is in a continual state of becoming.

Surely then, pandemonium offers a theme which is potentially rich in aesthetic, historical and cultural references. Moreover, with sleight of hand and an element of ludic typography, I would like to present a more complex, layered concept, for exploration—***Pan*-demonium**. Maybe ***Pan*-demonium** offers a metaphor for a critique of global capitalism and its 'devils'—its *pan*-demons—in all their guises, current *pan*-demics and moral *pan*-ics included? Perhaps it conjures up collective

[6] See Tamsin Lorraine, *Irigaray and Deleuze - Experiments in Visceral Philosophy*, Cornell Press, 1999, p. 140

creative forces—such as the anarchic Clown Army [7]—capable yet of mustering a political challenge? Might ***Pan*-demonium** even re-inscribe Great Pan—the lascivious piper-God, the woodland spirit, the solitary wanderer in the wilderness of night and instigator of *pan*ic—into a possibly productive contemporary mythology?

Adopting an ethic and aesthetic of the 'makeshift', ***bricolagekitchen*** invited visual, sonic and written responses to some of these ideas and questions. Through an exploration of the multiple meanings, interpretations and understandings of ***Pan*-demonium**, this exhibition, and the broader project it initiates, hopes to open up political as well as aesthetic potentialities. [8] At AC Institute in New York, it brings together an assembled cacophony of over fifty contemporary artistic responses and global voices gleaned via the web in a *pan*orama of sound, text, visual and moving

---

[7] See CIRCA, the clandestine insurgent rebel clown army, at www.clownarmy.org
[8] The project will continue to evolve via www.bricolagekitchen.com and through a viral imaging project, creating new communities at the interface of the ephemeral and the physical.

imagery, celebrating the *affective* power of disorder, *noise* and mess in an interactive presentation and an ongoing brico*logue*[9] of responses.

Bricolage, sieve orders and the ethics and aesthetics of mess

> Things *extra* and *other* (details and excesses coming from elsewhere) insert themselves into the accepted framework, the imposed order. The surface of this order is everywhere punched and torn open by ellipses, drifts, and leaks of meaning: it is a sieve-order.[10]

This project is part of a broader set of practices which engage with the notion of *bricolage*, a French term which has various histories and contexts. Most notable, perhaps, is Claude Lévi-Strauss who used it in the context of structuralist

---

[9] My hybrid term brings together the idea of *bricolage* (juxtaposition/makeshift/do-it-yourself) and *dialogue*.

[10] Michel de Certeau, *The Practices of Everyday Life*, (trans. Steven Rendall), [first published 1984], Berkeley/Los Angeles and London: University of California Press,1984, p.107

anthropology, referring in his 1966 classic study, *The Savage Mind*, to the *bricoleur* as 'a jack of all trades or a kind of professional do-it-yourself person.'[11]

In his seminal book, *The Practices of Everyday Life*, Michel de Certeau explores *bricolage* at length, referring to it as '....the dispersed, tactical and makeshift creativity of groups or individuals already caught in the nets of discipline...'[12] For de Certeau, 'makeshift creativity'—*bricolage*—is one of the procedures and ruses which compose the network of an 'antidiscipline'. Thus, *bricolage* is an improvisatory mode of making and doing, a practice which is multiform and fragmentary, non-conformist, delinquent and diversionary.

More recently, Steven Connor and others have identified *bricolage* as a key characteristic of postmodern culture which brings together a diverse spectrum of objects and ideas across a range of registers. In art practice, the old hierarchies about materials and value no longer have relevance: anything goes. More

---

[11] See Claude Lévi-Strauss, *The Savage Mind*, 1966, p.17.
[12] De Certeau, op.cit., p. xiv-xv.

significantly, the accommodation of low-tech and re-use approaches to artistic production and curation have ethical and ecological aspects with which this project —***Pan*-demonium**—has sought to engage.

Alongside the notion that cultural and textural production have a multiplicity of meanings and are subject to a plurality of interpretations, de Certeau's leaky 'sieve order' also lurks behind the project. For Deleuze and Guatari, there is no fixity and everything is in a state of infinite becoming

> The world has lost its pivot; the subject can no longer even dichotomize, but accedes to a higher unity, of ambivalence or overdetermination, in an always supplementary dimension to that of its object. The world has become chaos...[13]

[13] Gilles Deleuze and Félix Guattari, *A Thousand Plateaus, Capitalism and Schizophrenia* [1980], London: Continuum, 2004, p. 7

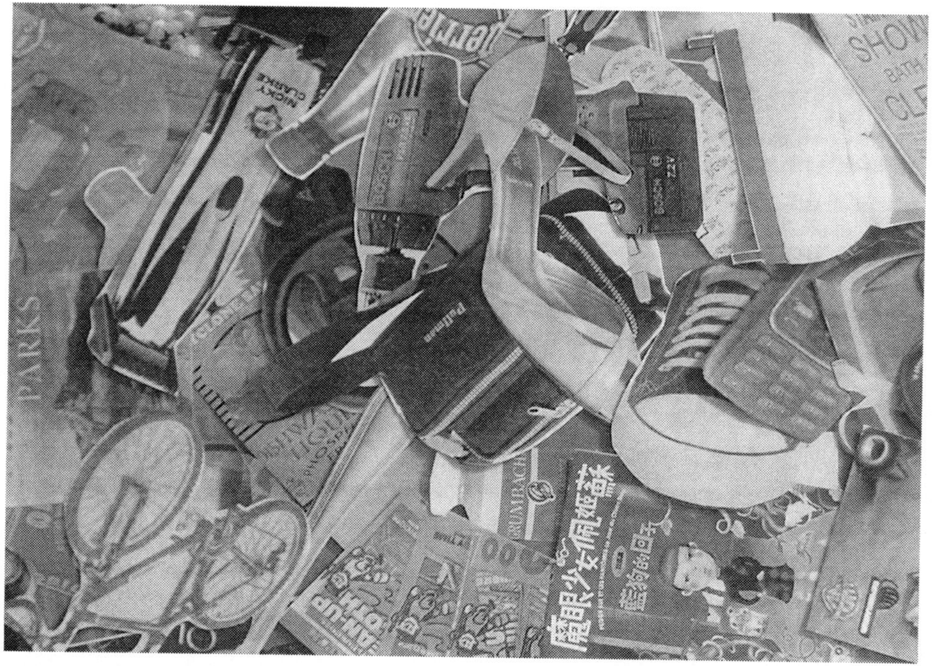

Elizabeth Gower
Can't remember where I put it
installation, detail
2009
photo:
bricolagekitchen

Living with the level of indeterminacy suggested here can be unsettling but is no more than an acknowledgement of the contingency of meaning and the lack of orderliness in the empirical world of things 'out there'. Indeed, Michel Serres writes about 'fuzzy logic' signifying a spectrum, a band, a continuum.

> Mathematicians call this new rigor "fuzzy": fuzzy subsets, fuzzy topology. They should be thanked: we have needed this fuzziness for centuries. While waiting for it, we seem to be playing the piano with boxing gloves on, in our world of stiff logic with our broad concepts.[14]

Elsewhere, with a fresh apprehension of the world of things and structures as complex and diffuse, 'mess' is increasingly being cited as a new paradigm in research methodology and is being transposed to other disciplines and creative practices. [15]

---

[14] Lawrence Schehr translates the French *flou*, meaning nebulous or blurry, as 'fuzzy' in Michel Serres, *Parasite*, p 56-7

[15] See John Law, *After Method, Mess in Social Science Research*, London/New York: Routledge, 2004

So whilst ***Pan*-demonium** collates and curates—with all the selective processes that involves—it attempts to work with some of these concepts. And, in the spirit of Deleuze and Guatari, aims to form a *rhizome*—setting down multiple roots and ceaselessly establishing connections - *within* the world. [16]

Pandemonium, politics and the public sphere

> The global is up for grabs. Globalization is simultaneously at its maximum and the globe at its nadir. There are lots of *blogs* but no globe. [17]

This project is staged in the city which was the locus of one of the most dramatic moments of pandemonium of the new century. Coincidentally, it emerges amidst the current Swine Flu pandemic: in a sci-fi scenario, the world's media issue daily

---

[16] Deleuze and Guatari, op.cit. p. 7

[17] Bruno Latour, 'From Realpolitik to Dingpolitik' in Bruno Latour and Peter Weibel (eds) *Making Things Public, Atmospheres of Democracy*, Karlsruhe/London: ZKM/MIT, 2005, p. 37

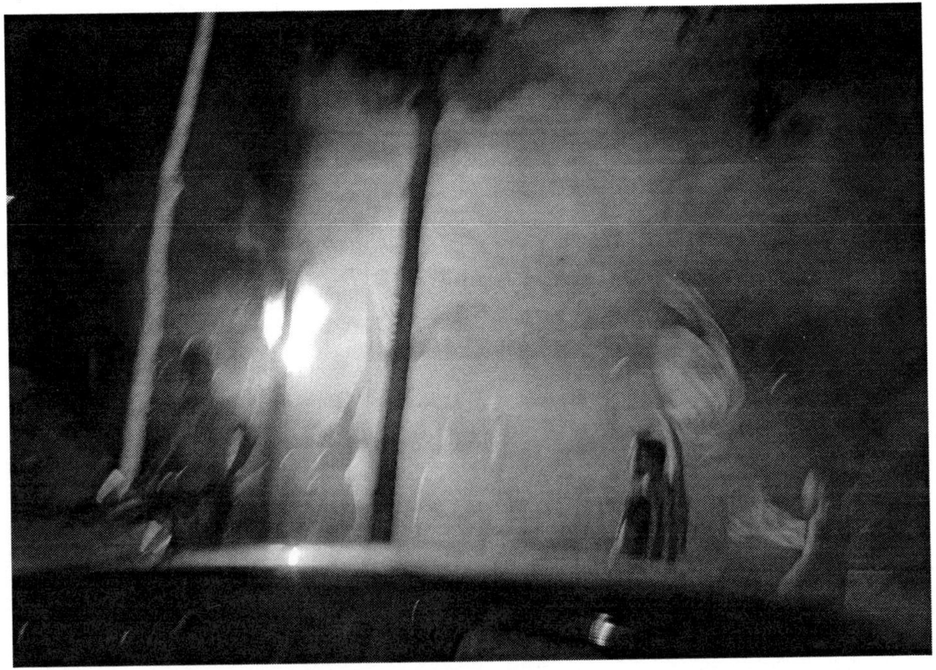

Gul Rose Smil
Mass Hysteria
Istanbul
2009
photograph

statistics and alarming predictions, spreading global panic about a virus out of control. Such events and scenarios engender fear and unleash processes of *demon*-isation.

In a post-9/11 context, in *Making Things Public*, Bruno Latour points out that, through an amazing quirk of etymology, the same root has given birth to both *Demon* and *Demos*—now, more at war with each other than Eteocles and Polynices ever were. [18] For Latour, demons constantly haunt politics—when the knife hovers around the 'cake of commonwealth', it either lets loose the 'demon of strife' or lets the 'demos be happily apportioned'. Creating its own pandemonium, for Latour, his project revealed not the *demon* of division but the *demon*, and fallacy, of unity, totality, transparency and immediacy.

Hence, in my view, there needs to be an acknowledgment that the public sphere viewed as a space of conflict, disruption and difference, can be positive and

---

[18] Latour, op.cit., p. 24.

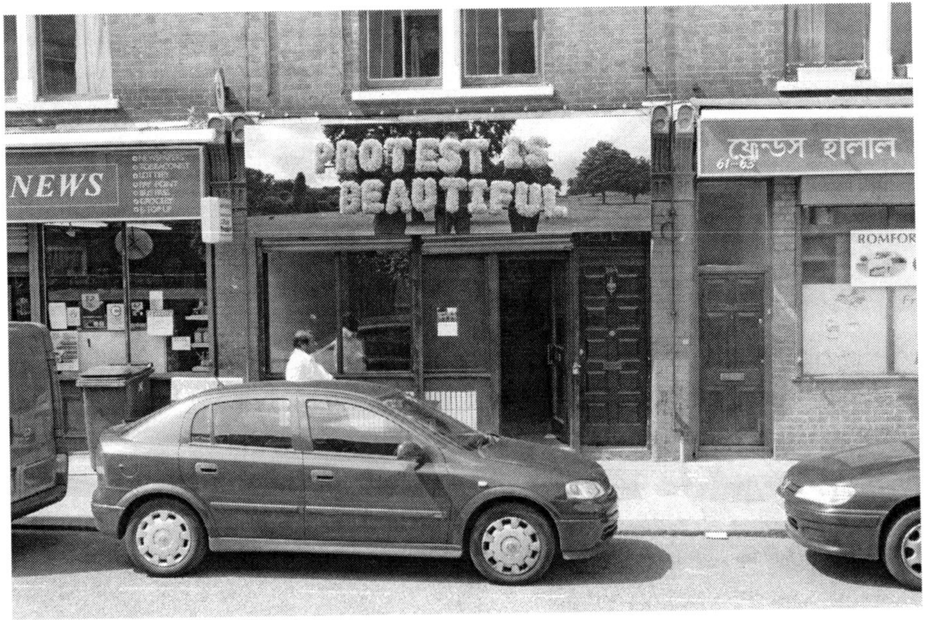

Freee
Protest is
Beautiful
1000,000PH
Gallery Façade
2007
photo:Andy
Hewitt

productive. Difference can be constructive and destructive but, most importantly, it engenders dialogue. Indeed, as Chantal Mouffe asserts, public space is not a space of consensus but is, essentially, a plurality of spaces of agonistic confrontation. [19] Failing to agree, as Hewitt and Jordan argue, is a fundamental strategy which they adopt to 'examine and attempt to reveal the inequalities and divisions within cultural systems'. [20] Critical artistic practices—such as Lemeh42's *New Italians* project [21]—can play an important role in subverting the dominant hegemony in this agonistic model of public space.

The global is 'up for grabs' but 'I fail to agree' entirely with Latour. It *is* possible to create 'globes', even if only in the form of temporary *pan* communities, such as the nascent one here in ***Pan*-demonium**. Critical artistic and cultural practice can both act *in* and have an effect *on* the real world, and it can also be *affective* too.

---

[19] Chantal Mouffe, p 104 – check in Moscow

[20] Hewitt + Jordan, *I Fail to Agree*, Site Gallery, Sheffield, 2004, p. 22. See Freee Collective, *Revolution is Sublime*, 2009 and www.freeecollective.com

[21] See Lemeh42, *New Italians: We Are All the Same*, 2009, animation wwwlemeh42indivia.net/

Noise

> Victory to the powers of noise; victory to the parasites, to all the parasites.....to those who will produce an indescribable clamor; to those who destroy the system they feed on, by multiplying. And finally, disorder reigns, by infection, by depletion of stocks and by noise ... [22]

> Every sound masks an entire history of sound, a cacophony of silence. Even our bodies hum along with the noise of the universe. In this complete history of sound, this cosmic echo which constitutes noise, sounds are not distinguished one from the next. Noise is the inarticulate, the confused mass of vibration in which sound relaxes or dissipates. [23]

---

[22] Michel Serres, *The Parasite*, (trans. L.R. Schehr), Minneapolis/London: University of Minnesota Press, [orig. published as *Le Parasite*, Grasset & Fasquelle, 1980], 2007, p. 250.

[23] Aden Evens, in Brian Massumi (ed) *A Shock to Thought: Expressions After Deleuze and Guattari*, London: Routledge, 2002, p.177

Noise has enormous affective potential. Ambient noise induces the body to relax whilst babies often sleep through deafeningly loud thrashing punk. Noise annoys and it invigorates. Michel Serres places *noise* at the centre of his episodic, mercurial writings—which are a form of noise in themselves. Cary Wolfe describes his writings as not analytical but experimental, not cumulative and aggregative but discursive, not linear but meandering, constantly doubling back on itself.

> And then we are plunged back into the welter, back into the complexity of it all. Back into the sea foam of noise. [24]

But Serres' notion of noise is complex. Noise—as static or interference - is one of the meanings of the French word parasite. For Serres, therefore, noise has a technological, informational element but it is, primarily, creative and productive. His

---

[24] Cary Wolfe, 'Introduction: Bring the Noise: The Parasite and the Multiple Genealogies of Posthumanism' in Serres, op.cit., p. xiii.

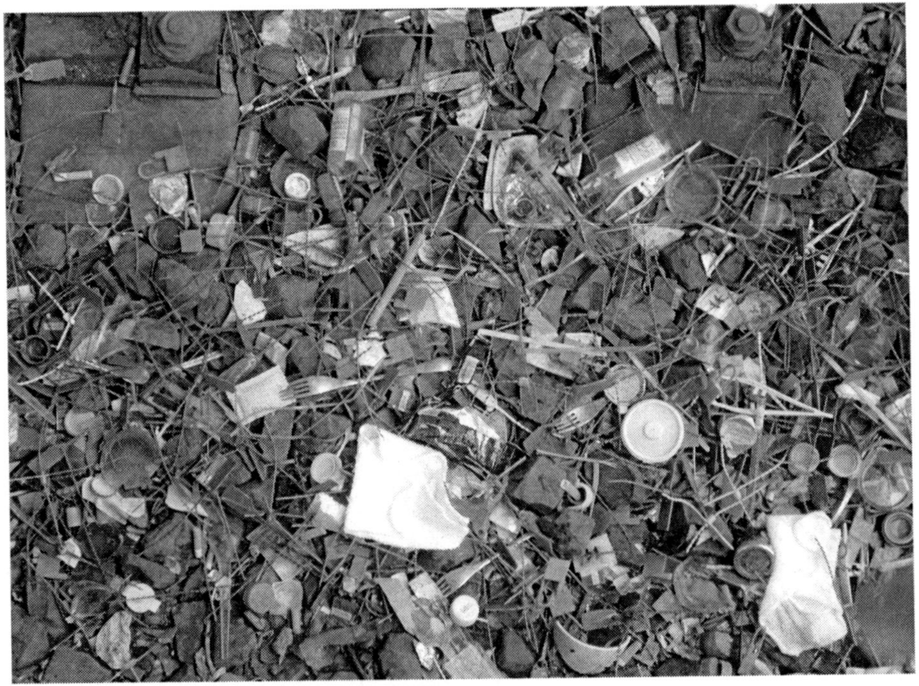

Briony Barr
On Train Tracks
2009
digital
photograph

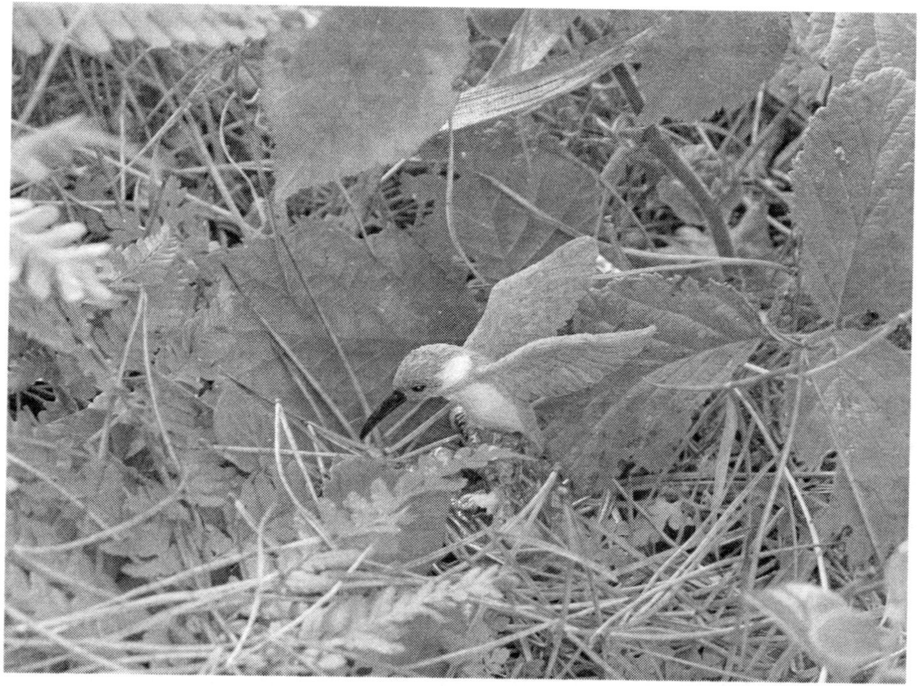

Lisa Stansbie
The Messenger
2008
digital still from
video

text, *The Parasite*, resounds with the crackling tongues of fire, the scratching of rodents, swarming fevers, barbaric rumblings, sonorous echoes, rackets and din.

If Serres' apprehension of productive noise is married to the practices and methodology of improvisation, we might ask if such explorations of indeterminacy can be *affective* in any political sense? Or, as Gary Peters suggests, might improvisation merely be the re-hashing of the given? [25] John Cage explored the boundaries of randomness and order extensively through his work. The distinction between order and disorder is paper-thin and border-crossings proliferate in live improvisation. Peters draws on Deleuze, understanding the improvisational process in the sense of 'nomadism' and 'infinite becoming'. Through this form of making and creating, an intensity of affect evokes, for me, a potentiality which speaks to a form of the political.

[25] See Gary Peters, *The Philosophy of Improvisation*, Chicago/London: University of Chicago Press, 2009, p. 4.

> The nomad is not necessarily one who moves: some voyages take place in situ, are trips in intensity...the journey is a motionless one,...it occurs on the spot, imperceptible, unexpected and subterranean... [26]

Great Pan is dead! Long live Pan!

> ....the rustic deity Pan, an Arcadian god of shepherds and goatherds...usually pictured as being part-human in form and part-goat with the horns, ears and legs of the latter; and he was goatish in character too, for he was lustful and sportive, a vigorous and fertile nature-spirit who could also be short-tempered, especially if disturbed from his noontide rest. A characteristic power of his...is that of causing 'panic', a wild groundless fear that strikes groups of people and causes them to behave like frightened stampeded animals. [27]

Plutarch, a priest at Delphi in the first century A.D., recounted the story about the news of Great Pan's death, noting that a hundred years later, Pan's shrines, altars

---

[26] Deleuze quoted in Peters, op.cit., p. 150.
[27] Robin Hard, *The Routledge Handbook of Greek Mythology*, London: Routledge, 2004, p. 214.

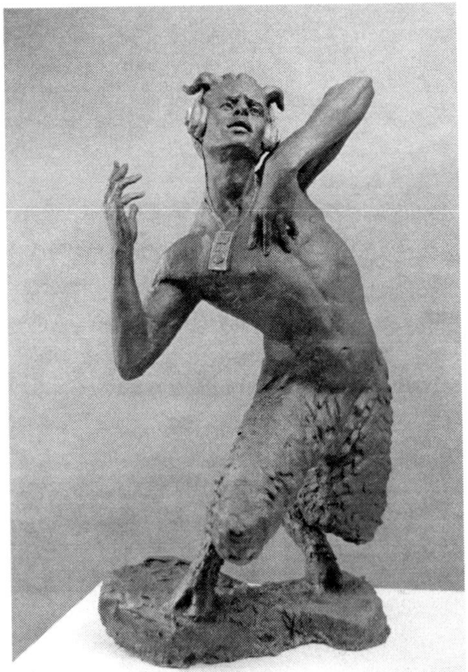

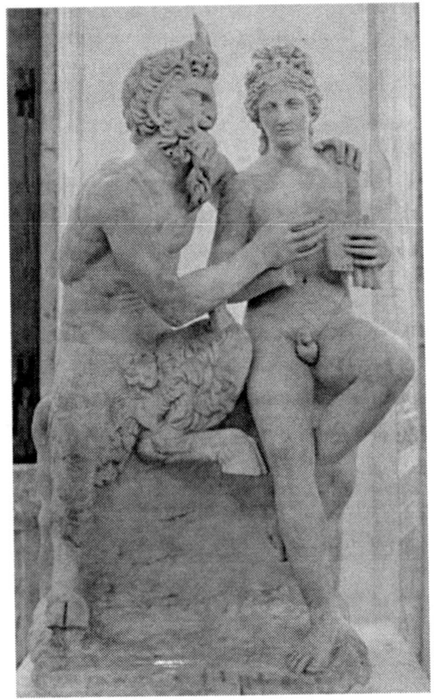

left
Adam Reeder,
Pan with his iPod
2008, bronze

right
Pan teaching Daphnis to play pipes
Heliodorus of Rhodes (copy)
photo: Jastrow

sacred caves and mountains were still much frequented. [28] With a revival of pantheism through a contemporary phase of New Age eco-spirituality, maybe Pan is not dead. Perhaps, besides lingering on in wooded groves, gardens and allotments, he also loiters in the cosmopolis. Pan is playing in the multi-storey car parks, on the pavements, behind the lamp-posts, across the internet.

Perhaps Pan is alive and kicking, though not necessarily making a racket.
Noise does not have to be loud, there are other ways to 'speak'. As Paul Virilio notes, the Futurists called for people to sing and shout, to deafen people with triumphant fanfares of din and noise-making machines. From the end of the 1920s, silence was put 'on trial' as, from that moment, 'whoever says nothing is deemed to consent'. [29]

---

[28] According to Graves who, despite the rather dubious scholarship of his study, remains an important icon of the New Age - Robert Graves, *The Greek Myths:1,* [1955], Harmondsworth: Penguin, 1960, p. 102

[29] Paul Virilio, *Art and Fear*, [2000], London/New York: Continuum, 2004, p. 74.

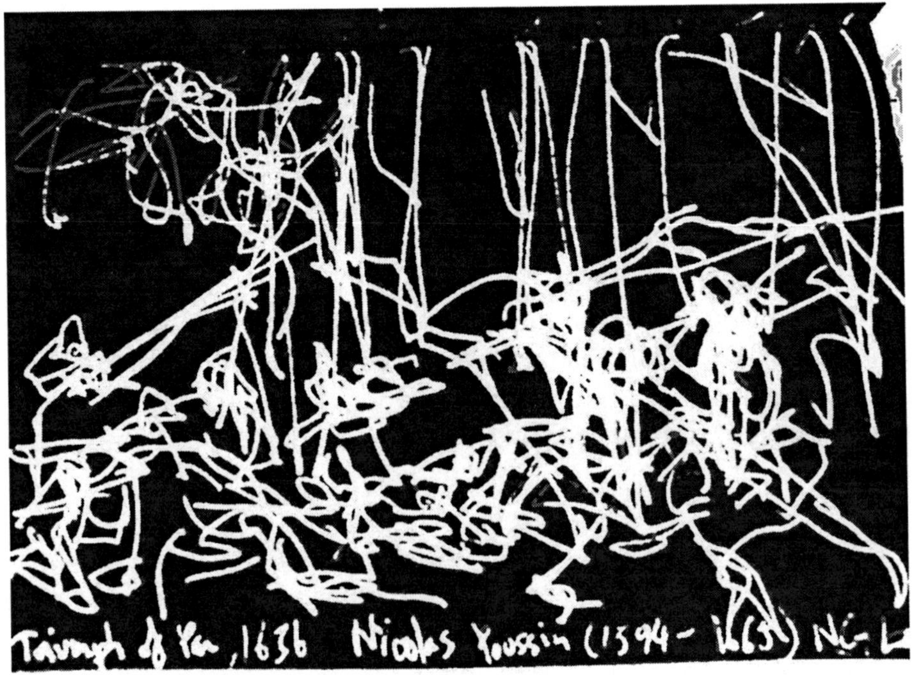

Kim Wan
Pan study after Poussin
2009
drawing

> ...those that SHOUT and SCREAM—their pain or hate—would soon abolish all dialogue and rule out any form of questioning...[30]

Virilio reminds us that we have all become terrified of silence and must rethink it. Certainly, silence can have profound aesthetic and political weight; witness the 'silent protests' of the tens of thousands of demonstrators who marched through the streets of Tehran in June 2009, in a direct challenge to the authority of Iran's clerical regime.

So ***Pan*-demonium** goes on. In all its forms and guises, Pan proliferates surreptitiously, flitting and 'twittering' across the web, playing quietly in the streets, creating temporary networks and dialogic communities, sowing the disruptive seeds of production and creativity across the globe. Great Pan is Dead! Long live Pan!

---

[30] Ibid., p. 91 and see p. 86.

bricolagekitchen aka Gillian Whiteley is an interdisciplinary artist-curator-writer working across critical-creative borders, currently based at Loughborough University School of Art and Design, UK. Her wide-ranging creative/research interests have a focus on the use of 'trash' in visual/material culture and improvisational and collaborative practices. She has researched, published and curated a number of projects linking art and bricolage, junk assemblage and the politics of the social, public and *affective* imagination. Exhibitions include *Radical Mayhem: Welfare State International and its Followers* (UK, 2008), related forthcoming publications include *Junk : Art and the Politics of Trash* (IB Tauris), *Scavenging from margins to mainstream? Artist as Bricoleur in the 21st Century* (University of Paris) and the co-edited *Telling Stories: Countering Narrative in Art,Theory and Film* (2009). The ***Pan-*** **demonium** project is part of her ongoing research into bricolage and improvisatory techniques as a paradigm for research and practice. www.bricolagekitchen.com

Artists and contributors to *Pan*-demonium at AC Institute NYC

Abstractus

Based Colombia

Synthetic Dream's Garden: Harvest hidden behind the insatiable gluttony 2009

Synthetic Dream's Garden: Disturbing blossoming accumulations 2009

Two photo installations

Ximena Steevens and Mauricio Velez have worked together since 2002 as an artist duet known as Abstractus. They 'present human existence as a paradoxical fact' as the core of their work. Through art they assert that they 'try to kill this fucking alienation that we all love so much, while unsustainable future is under construction by careless insiders in this impassive chaos'. www.abstractusart.com

Adam Burton

Based UK
Acceptable Answers (Greyboards) 2008-2009
Three text panels

Adam Burton completed his MFA at Bath Spa University in 2007. He lives and works in London. His work is concerned with provoking a political reaction in others and seeing whether or not this is possible. His work is also about exploring his own beliefs. Recent exhibitions include Meantime Project Space, Cheltenham and *EASTinternationa*l 2009 at Norwich. www.adamburton.com/

Andrew Erdos

Based USA
SANTALOPE, YOU CAN'T KEEP US OUT! photo by Julianne Zimmerman 2008
SANTALOPE, UNINVITED PERFORMANCE @ ART BASEL MIAMI BEACH! photo by Lee Wells 2008
SANTALOPE, ADDICTED TO INK! photo by Stephanie Sea 2008
Series photoprints

New York based artist Andrew Erdos combines sculpture, video, performance, photography and installation to create a humorous and bizarre spectacle embracing the absurdity of globalization, western cultural imperialism, and ravenous consumerism. In the last two years Erdos has participated in over 30 exhibitions on 5 continents. He has shown at venues such as The National Centre for Contemporary Art (Moscow), Beijing BS1 Contemporary Art Center, The Chelsea Art Museum (New York), and was included in the 2008 Deitch Projects Art Parade. More of his work can be seen at www.SANTALOPE.com

Andy Clover

Based New Zealand
End This Night 2009
Audio 5mins

Andy Clover was born in Wellington and lives and works in New Zealand. He is an artist who works with ideas, mining the recesses of his mind for old impulses or long forgotten memories and combining them with incoming strands from a multitude of other sources. Like many artists of his generation, his work is unavoidably influenced by the mass media and popular culture, but also draws references from literature, overheard conversations, graffiti and art theory. Clover enjoys the freedoms of post-modernity and works in numerous media including computer-generated graphics, drawing, light, painting and installation. www.andyclover.com

Anne Kolin

Based France
Wall Street Trader 2009
Justice Sociale 2009

Anne Kolin was born in Paris and became interested in modern art while living in Amsterdam between 1982 and 1988. A frequent visitor to the Stedelijk Museum, she was particularly inspired by the work of Karel Appel and the *Grande Parade* exhibition of 1986. On her return to Paris, Anne Kolin obtained a Masters Degree in plastic arts at La Sorbonne, where her work was heavily influenced by the paintings of Bacon, Picasso and Giacometti. Recent exhibitions include Noho Gallery, Chelsea, New York. www.annekolin.com

Barnaby Dicker

Based UK
Pan is written on the blank page 2009
Text

Barnaby Dicker is a filmmaker and an academic currently completing a PhD on Frame-Based Cinematography at Royal Holloway, University of London. Conceptions of filmmaking as a mixed- or inter-media, collaborative and/or documentary practice underpin his work. Research interests also include: 'proto-' and early cinematography; the cinematographic 'imaginary' and para-cinematographic practices; 'counter-' and 'anti-' cinema. He lives in Swansea with his wife and two children.

Beatrix Ward-Fernandez/Charlie Collins

Based UK
Castillo de Luna 2009
Audio, theremin and waterphone 14mins 47 secs

Beatrix Ward-Fernandez was born in London and raised in Cadiz, Southern Spain. She has classical violin training but her interest in creative/improvised musics led to the theremin and its use within acoustic/experimental ensembles. Over the past few years she has recorded/performed with a large number of creative artists, including Mick Beck, Pat Thomas, J.D. Parran, Jez Riley French, Pleasure-Drenching Improvers, Paul Dunmall, Chris Corsano and Okkyung Lee. In July 2007 her trio performed at the theremin symposium *Hands Off.* Her music has been released on *Discus, Found Property* and *Singing Knives*.www.myspace.com/beatrixwardfernandez

Charlie Collins has played improvised music since 1969, RnB/free jazz through the 1970s, and by 1978 was involved in the nascent "Industrial" scene, recording for cult labels *Industrial, Fetish* and *Doublevision*, and the first releases on the legendary *Go!Discs.* Over the last 20 years he has toured/recorded throughout Europe, in regular groups and ad-hoc ensembles, received numerous awards for live performance and composition, worked with dance groups, taught improvisation and toured a live soundtrack to Teinosuke Kinugasa's silent masterpiece *A Page of Madness.* Since 2007 he has been a member of Sonny Simmons UK-based quartet and performs with Ted Daniel/Michael Marcus in *Duology + 2*. He remains one of a handful of musicians to have played Derek Bailey's *Company*. www.myspace.com/charlievibe

Beck/Bright/Jasnoch

Based UK

May Day! May Day! The Devil's Out of the Bottle 2008

Live recording at Heeley Institute, Sheffield, 1 May 208

Audio 11mins

Mick Beck is a free-player on saxophones and bassoon, an improvising big band leader and instigator of many unique experimental music projects. His technical innovations and musical ideas are a source of inspiration to his collaborators. His collective *FeetPackets* was influential in the late 1980s and in the 1990s he led various small groups including *Something Else* with Paul Hession and Simon Fell. Based in Sheffield, he plays regularly in London and also Spain, Germany, Austria, Canada and Australia. He has worked with numerous musicians including Derek Bailey, Tony Buck and Rainer Kuhn. http://www.efi.group.shef.ac.uk/mbeck.html

Geoff Bright is a free-playing improviser on soprano, alto, tenor saxophone and primal scream. He develops improvising projects in partnership with other musicians under the name *Racket Tackle*. He is also interested in improvisation as a research methodology in critical social research.

John Jasnoch plays various guitars (electric, acoustic, fretless baritone, soprano 12 string, lap steel) and mandolin. He became part of *Sheffield Free Music Group* and the free jazz-rock group *Bass Tone Tap* in the 1970s and was in *Company Week* in 1988. He has partnered many free-players and taken part in various adhoc groups of improvisers including the *Modun Quarte*t and the *Bone Orchestra*, playing across Europe and North America. http://www.myspace.com/johnjasnoch

The trio are part of *The Gated Community*, an ever-changing collective of improvisors set up by Mick Beck in 2005. http://www.freenoise.co.uk/artists/gated_community.htm

Branka Vidovic-Butler

Based UK
Human Rights 2009
text

Branka Vidovic-Butler is an anthropologist, artist and professional exile. Born in Bosnia, raised in Croatia where, due to the Balkan War, she was exiled with her family to Sweden as political refugees. She now lives and works in England with her English husband and four rescue cats. As an artist, she tries to inhabit a vision of a life that is her own rather than

being subjected to other people's notion of what 'normality' is.
www.professionalexile.co.uk and brankavidovicbutler.blogspot.com/

Brian Rhodes

Based UK
Glenn Branca (Phase Shift)
Transmission (Phase Shift)
Video 7/10 mins loop

Brian Rhodes is a multimedia artist. He studied Fine Art at the University of Wolverhampton and Central Saint Martins, London. Exhibitions in 2009 include *Screenplay* at the James Taylor Gallery, London, *Transfixed Motion/The Transitory Still* at Sheffield Institute of Art and Design Gallery. In 2008, he showed work in Cologne, Hamburg, Spain and London.

Briony Barr

Based Australia
Cigarettes 2009
On Train Tracks 2009
Digital photographs

Briony Barr makes site-specific, installation-based work that explores line drawing as a system of movement and change. Her photographic work documents examples of process, motion, accumulation and convergence, observed in the course of everyday life. Barr's practice also involves interdisciplinary, collaborative work with scientists and children. She lives in Melbourne, Australia.

Charlene Clempson

Based UK
Debulge Kitchen 2009
The Hand of God 2009
Two photoprints

Charlene Clempson was born in Coventry, UK. She is a mixed media artist who completed her Masters Degree in Textile Print at Central Saint Martins, and is now working towards a Ph.D in Art at Loughborough University. She explores personal and cultural identity in search of a viewer's inner longing. She has exhibited in the UK and Europe and her work is in several private collections. Charlene is currently working on a solo show and is artist in residence at CEIMH (Centre of Excellence in Interdisciplinary Mental Health Birmingham University, UK).

Corpus Collective

Based USA
Perpetual Madscene 2009
Video 5mins 10secs

The Corpus Collective are Ektoras Binikos, William Brovelli, Avi Rosen and Anna Viola Hallberg. FERALISM is their approach to work in which individual boundaries are blurred and personal content, be it physical or intellectual, is unleashed to move through an exchange of hands, moving it from a static domesticated state to an active feral state, thus opening it up to numerous creative possibilities. The Corpus Collective is a conceptual and process-based endeavor which aims to establish a vortex of creative energy and ideas that will challenge the notion of the singular creative voice and practice, by multiplying that voice throughout a collective effort. www.artdoxa.com/users/corpuscollective

David Berridge

Based UK

GAME, GLOBAL, GREEN, GROWN, GUYS 2009

Text

David Berridge's work involves writing and using language in a variety of settings, including galleries, print, online, teaching and performance. It includes online artist projects for *Refutation*; critical writings on experimental art and ecology for the RSA *Art &Ecology* magazine; collaborative performances/lectures at Project Arts Centre, Dublin and Plan 9, Bristol; workshops on experimental essaying for KOMPLOT, Brussels; and a script for an exhibition at TOTALKUNST gallery, Edinburgh, in 2010. He is particularly interested in the history and contemporary practice of different forms of scores and notations, and in the methodologies for research and group processes that emerge from histories of experimental art. He edits/writes the blogzine *More Milk Yvette: A Journal of the Broken Screen* at www.moremilkyvette.blogspot.com. Also see soanyway.org.uk/davidberridge.htm

David Clarke

Based Hong Kong
Urbanyoga 2009
Text
Screaming escalator 2009
Found sound, audio

David Clarke grew up in Devon, England, and studied at the University of London. Since 1986, he has lived in Hong Kong, where he is currently Professor in the Department of Fine Arts, University of Hong Kong. He has published a number of books, most recently two photo books about Hong Kong: *Reclaimed Land: Hong Kong in Transition* (Hong Kong University Press, 2002) and *Hong Kong x 24 x 365: A Year in the Life of a City* (Hong Kong University Press, 2007). His most recent one-person exhibition was *Hong Kong Experience: An Exhibition of Photographs* by David Clarke, held at the Brewhouse Gallery, Royal William Yard, Plymouth, England, 9-24 March 2007.
www.fa.hku.hk/DavidClarkePortfolio/index.htm

David Tucker

Based UK
Krek! 2009
Audio/text 2mins loop

David Tucker is an Associate Tutor in English at the University of Sussex UK where he researches the work of Samuel Beckett. He has previous and forthcoming publications on Beckett, and has participated in a number of musical projects and collaborations. *KREK!* is part of a larger project involving recordings of songs and musical pieces written by Beckett in published works and manuscripts.

Dhaleen Devenish-Bright

Based UK
Pan 2009
Viral image

Dhaleen Devenish-Bright is an independent artist-illustrator with an Anglo-Thai background with interests in audio and visual art forms. She is inspired by psychedelic art, ancient mythologies and contemporary multiculturalism. Despite the rise in global consumerism, she believes the individual can still have a voice in the ongoing debate. For her, the way forward is to balance nature with humanity for the cultivation of a deeper egalitarian society.

Elizabeth Gower

Based Australia
Can't remember where I put it 2009
Found materials installation

Elizabeth Gower has had over 30 one-person exhibitions throughout Australia as well as London, Sharjah and New York, most recently exhibiting in 2009 at AC (Institute Direct Chapel) in New York, Longwood University, Virginia and Bevard Art Museum, Florida. She has been the recipient of numerous grants from the Australia Council, Victorian Ministry for the Arts and NETS Victoria as well as awarded Alliance Française Art Fellowship, Australian Postgraduate Award and residencies at Cité Internationale des Arts in Paris and the Australia Council studios at Paretaio Italy, Barcelona and New York.
www.elizabethgower.com

Fabienne Audéoud

Based France
Sisters 2009
Video 5mins

Fabienne Audéoud is a performance artist/musician who has shown across the most eclectic scenes worldwide, from opera stages to clubs, galleries and museums. Before moving from London to Paris, Audéoud traveled several times to Senegal where she was deeply moved by people's approach to music. In 2001 she won the Belfast Ormeau Bath Gallery Award for a performance which toured to London, Istanbul, Brussels, Amsterdam and Stockholm. Since 2000 she has collaborated with John Russell, founding member of the artists' group BANK. Their collaborative work was shown in many solo shows including *The Withdrawal from Conversation; The Return to the Oceanic / The Weight of the Breast: Twenty Women Play the Drums Topless*, South London Gallery. Group shows include White Columns, New York; Galerie desTerreaux, Musée d'Art Contemporain de Lyon; Tate Modern, London; 'Becks Futures 2', ICA, London; Fruitmarket Gallery, Edinburgh.

Freee

Based UK

Revolution is Sublime 2009

Installation, printed balloons

Freee is a collective made up of three artists, Dave Beech, Andy Hewitt and Mel Jordan, who work together on slogans, performances, billboards and publications that challenge the commercial and bureaucratic colonization of the public sphere of opinion formation. Freee occupies the public sphere with works that take sides, speak their mind and divide opinion. www.freee.org.uk

Georgia Kotretsos

Based USA

Rambo is missing his brothers! January 7th 2009

Blog Text

Georgia Kotretsos was born in Thessaloniki, Greece. She attained an MFA Degree from The School of the Art Institute of Chicago and a BFA Degree from The Durban Institute of Technology, in KwaZulu Natal, (2000) in South Africa. Kotretsos is a founding agent of the

Boots Contemporary Art Space, St. Louis MO, USA and the founder/editor-in-chief of *Boot Print,* a publication dedicated to contemporary art www.bootsart.com. By challenging conceptual boundaries, authorship and authority, she has created a body of work that is characterized by its conceptual consistency. She has exhibited in South Africa, the United States, and Europe and also writes for the *Art in the Twenty-First Century* blog in New York where she has a regular monthly column called Inside the Artist's Studio.
blog.art21.org/author/georgia-kotretsos/

Graham Scott

Based UK
Kabaret/Wroclaw/Berlin 2009
Interactive décollage installation

Graham Scott is a visual artist who studied Fine Art in Newcastle, Nottingham and Birmingham in the UK. He is currently working on a series of paintings based upon fragments of text and ephemera found on walls and hoardings and material from photographs taken in Nottingham, Paris, Berlin and Wroclaw. The resulting work utilises the accidental/random nature of the material and the arbitrary juxtapositions of text and imagery, and provides the opportunity to exploit both figurative and abstract qualities found in the urban landscape. In keeping with a bricolage and improvisatory ethic, this interactive piece invites viewers to engage in *décollage* and create new work.

Gul Rose Smil

Based USA

Mass Hysteria, SISTA BLISS, Madness of Crowds, Istanbul June 2009

Series of photograph prints

Gul Kozacioglu, aka GUL ROSE SMIL is a conceptual-performance artist born in Turkey, raised in Denmark and France. Currently based in New York, developing an internet performance MUSE ME with participants and audience spatially located across continents. She works in collaborative practice under the name of CELEB-RATION, together with an adhoc group of artists that come together for larger projects. Her performative projects reject boundaries - especially national and audience/artist - and try to eliminate these in participatory work, utilizing internet, sms messages, projections, media screens, and public space to bridge together art and community. MUSE ME is supported by Anadolu Kultur. GUL = ROSE = SMIL www.gulkozacioglu.com

Henry Gwiazda

Based USA
Butterfingerbutterfinger 2009
Audio 1min 1 sec
Afterglow 1990
Audio 8mins

Henry Gwiazda is a new media artist/composer whose artistic trajectory has taken him from sampling, sound effects and immersive technologies to his current work with new media. This new work is a comprehensive artistic approach that is multimedia in nature and focused on movement. His works are regularly screened in festivals and galleries throughout the world including New York, Paris, Madrid, Cairo, Amsterdam, Beijing, Naples, Marseilles, Damascus, Athens, Istanbul. In 2008, he won First Prize at Abstracta Cinema in Rome and this year, Second Prize at the Crosstalk Video Art Festival in Budapest.
www.henrygwiazda.com

Jeremy Newman

Based USA

The Vase 2008

Video 1min

Jeremy Newman has directed numerous experimental and documentary videos. His work is frequently shown at film festivals including the Detroit Docs International Film Festival, the Panorama of Independent Film Makers in Greece, and the Tribeca Underground Film Festival and has also aired on several PBS stations. He is Assistant Professor of Communications at The Richard Stockton College of New Jersey. Newman has an MFA from The Ohio State University.

Javier Seco

Based Spain

Muy Fragil

Oil

1968-2008

The Planet Goes

Be Careful

Balance
Series of photoprints

Javier Seco was born in San Sebastian and lives and works in Spain. He is a multimedia artist whose work maintains close ties with words and language through the creation of a kind of 'poetry of visual objects'. His art practice also encompasses actions, performances and installations. He belongs to the artist groups LIGHT AND CIA and PERMANENT MAGNETS and their environmental concerns are a constant theme in Seco's ironic works. His work has been exhibited extensively in Spain, across Europe, the USA, South America and Japan and his work features in various anthologies of visual poetry. www.javierseco.com www.tallerdelosentido.net

Jonny Drury

Based UK
The Average American sees three thousand advertisements a day 2009
Electronic audio 6mins 30secs

Jonny Drury is a multimedia artist and improvising musician. He is founder of *Freenoise*, an events company for live experimental music and is currently working towards his MA

Contemporary Art at Sheffield Hallam University, UK
www.freenoise.co.uk

Josef Bares

Based Czech Republic/China
txiaozhu.org / Tiananmen Remix 2006
video, 1min 5secs

Josef Bares was born in Prague. After receiving a degree in international business he started his studies at the Academy of Fine Arts in Prague where he is currently a graduate student. His focus is on media art, combining existing and emerging communication models. In his works, he deals with topics of human perception and communication on both individual and intercultural levels. He lives and works in Prague, but can be found in China quite often.

Kao Okada

Based Germany/Japan
One's Born Days
Video 2mins 30secs
A Trampin'
Video 5mins

Kao Okada is a multimedia performance artist, born in Japan and living and working in Dusseldorf, Germany and Okayama, Japan. She studied art in Stuttgart and Dusseldorf. She has exhibited work in Dusseldorf, Los Angeles and Kyoto.

Kim Wan

Based UK
Pan studies after Poussin and Boucher in the National Gallery collection, London 2009
Series of drawings, photoprints

Kim Wan, of Chinese–Malay descent, was educated at Winchester School of Art, UK. Kim Wan describes himself as an artist who 'makes' paintings, drawings and objects, that he imbues with a gestural and authentic finish. These build up over time to create new bodies

of work. Working on an international platform, Kim has an exhibition in 2009 in Beijing, China, and is representing the UK at the Florence Biennale in December 2009.
www.kimwanart.com

Krzysztof Topolski aka Arszyn

Based Poland
Folk Science 2009
Electronic audio 5 mins 57 secs

Krzysztof Topolski is a musician in the field of electronic and electroacoustic music. Under the alias Arszyn, he acts as a sound and multimedia artist, holds workshops on new music, listening and soundscape and has curated art and educational projects in the Centre of Contemporary Art _a_nia in Gda_sk. He explores percussive music, composing and performing electronic and electroacoustic, improvised and rock music and creates sound installations. He cooperates and occasionally performs with musicians/artists such as Tomasz Duda, M.bunio.S, Emiter, Tomasz Szwelnik, Muk, Thomas Lehn, Andrew Sharplay, Miko_aj Trzaska, Hoec, Dj Wojak, free103point9, Wojtek Mazolewski.
www.myspace.com/arszyn

Laura Wild

Based UK
Guided Tour Becoming Story 2009
Video 10mins 32secs

Laura Wild is studying for a PhD at Loughborough University in the UK, exploring how 'becoming' can be embodied as 'art' through ordinary activities, such as keeping and cultivating an allotment. For her, the allotment offers a metaphorical ground for the interment of the art object and a physical space for a reflexive practice of thinking through digging. Her work has been exhibited in the UK, including shows at Truro Cathedral, Newlyn Art Gallery and Williamson Tunnels, Liverpool. www.laurawild.blogspot.com/

Lemeh42

Based Italy
New Italians: We Are All The Same
Video 1min

Lemeh42 are Santini Michele (Degree in Foreign Literatures) and Paoloni Lorenza (Degree in Fine Arts). In 2009, Lemeh42 received first prizes for their video portfolios at ICEBERG,

Bologna, Italy, at FONLAD Digital Art Festival, Coimbra, Portugal and at MAGMART International Video Art Festival, CAM, Casoria, Napoli. In 2009, they showed work at Ars Virtua, Southern California Institute of Architecture, Los Angeles, USA and Salon de arte digital, Cologne and OFF IV, Maracaibo,Venezuela. They also showed work at the 809 International New Image Art Festival, Yichang City, China. lemeh42.indivia.net/

Lisa Erb (Laboratorium)

Based Germany

MMYSTER YRTEMMYS From To (live mix) 2008

Excerpt, audio

Opera Omnia 2009

Text

Lisa Erb lives and works in Munich, Germany. With a background in physics, maths and fine art, she combines these disciplines into installations as well as online and printed publications. Erb has held solo and group exhibitions in Amsterdam, Munich, Vienna and Dusseldorf and her work was included in the Berlin Biennale 2006. *MMYSTER YRTEMMYS* is one of Erb's music projects and is part of *LIFE/LOVE/Information Digestion Investigations, &*

Kulturmanagement Laboratorium Erb, a collaborative union of 'diversified-me' operators or real collaborators. www.lisaerb.com

Lisa Stansbie

Based UK
The Messenger 2008
Video 3 mins 10 secs

Lisa Stansbie is a multimedia artist who has undertaken residencies and shown across Europe and in the U.S. In 2007 she created a fictional digital archive for The Harris Museum, Preston and produced a film piece for the group exhibition *odoo/current* in Ulaanbaatar, Mongolia. Her films have been shown in The Athens Video Art Festival, Siberia International Film (London), The Olympolis Project (Pieria, Greece), Art Tech Media Festivals (Puerto de la Cruz, Tenerife/Cordoba, Spain) and Purescreen 2008 (Manchester UK). Her films were recently screened at University of Auckland Gallery as an online exhibition titled 'Hackamore' curated by Anna Parlane. 2009 exhibitions include The Text Festival, Bury U.K and a solo exhibition at VSG, London. She is joint editor (with Dr Derek Horton) of www.soanyway.org.uk a magazine project on approaches to narrative and storytelling. Also see her screenings at www.slashseconds.org.

Liz-n-Val

Based USA
Bird Twist 2008
Video 3 mins loop

The artist team Liz-N-Val have collaborated for over 25 years, using unorthodox materials, processes and concepts and their unmediated direct approach to Art-making and audiences is still not fully understood. Their unprecedented deployment of mass-media as an Art medium and distribution system and the use of non-traditional exhibition spaces expand individual possibilities and inspire many generations of Artists and cultural thinkers, world-wide. They are the creators of 'Abstractrealism', the philosophy of something from nothing Art. Abstractrealism is the logical outcome of Abstract Art and Realism. www.liz-n-val.net

Louise Marlborough/Olive Barrett

Based Ireland
Beat this 2009
Video 3mins 17secs

Louise Marlborough graduated in Fine Art/sculpture from the National College of Art and

Design in Dublin. In 2000, she studied photographic practices at the London College of Printing. Marlborough has been exhibiting work for the last ten years in solo and group exhibitions. She is a member of The Gallery of Photography in Dublin and has work in private collections in the UK, Ireland and Australia.

Olive Barrett studied at the National College of Art and Design in Dublin where she graduated in Textile Design and later specialized in Art and Design Education. Over the last 14 years, Barrett has exhibited nationally and internationally in solo, group shows and public art projects. In 2007, she received a commendation for her part in the Jameson Film Festival. She is a member of the Artists' Association in Ireland, IVARO and Artmesh.

Margarida Sardinha

Based Portugal
Hyper-self Light Dance 2009
Video 11 mins

Margarida Sardinha was born in Lisbon and studied at Central Saint Martins College of Art and Design and Chelsea College of Art and Design, London. She was on the exchange program with the L'Ecole Nationale Superieure d'Art de Cergy, Paris. She has shown work at the Bienal Jovens Valoures 09 in Portugal, 2009 and at Galeria Pedro Serrenho, Lisbon, 2009. She founded pARTart and with it curated the exhibition *London Recycled* at the Menier Chocolate Factory in London, 2004. She exhibited the solo show *Darkness Reflexions* at Casa Museu Fernando Pessoa in Lisbon, 2003-04 and participated in The Triangle Space Studios OPEN in London, 2003. She exhibited at Riverside Studios with the Artists in Exile group supported by the Arts Council in London, 2001 and was selected for the Network AD at the Candid Arts Trust Gallery in London, 2001. www.margaridasardinha.com

Maria Zhalnina

Based Russia/USA
Maps of the World 2009
Series photoprints of objects

Maria Zhalnina was born in Russia where she studied art at the Moscow State Academic Art Institute. She lives and works in Russia and the USA. She seeks to connect the conceptual and visual worlds, playing with popular stereotypes and sayings and considers herself to be a follower of the 'Moscow school of conceptualism'. Her work has been exhibited in Russia, the Netherlands and Bosnia/Herzegovina. Recent shows include the Fire Arts Festival, Oakland and the Burning Man Festival in Nevada, USA.

Mark Cooley

Based USA

PS4 2009

Interactive console game, playstation/tv

Mark Cooley is an interdisciplinary artist interested in exploring the intersections of art, activism, popular culture and institutional critique in a variety of contexts. Subjects of particular interest are US foreign policy, the fine art culture industry and the political economy of new technologies. Cooley's work has been featured internationally in online and offline venues such as Exit Art, NY, Rhizome.org, Furtherfield.org, the World Social Forum, MediaLabMadrid. He is currently a professor in the Department of Art and Visual Technology at George Mason University. www.flawedart.net

Martin Archer/Geoff Bright

Based UK

Angelus Novus 1-5, 2009

Audio 5 x 1mins

Since his move in the early 1990s from free jazz saxophonist to studio-based electronics composer, Martin Archer has produced a series of highly acclaimed CDs which combine electronics-based structures with written and improvised parts for brass, woodwind, strings and voices. Elements from jazz, free improvisation, contemporary classical music, electronica, and cutting edge rock music are all present within his work. As a performer, Archer seeks to avoid the inert and inexpressive performance style inherent in much live electronic music. www.discus-music.co.uk See Beck/Bright/Jasnoch for Geoff Bright.

Paolo Consorti

Based Italy
Beatitudes 1, 2 and 3, 2009
Inkjet on photopaper
Hell, 2008
Lambda print

Paolo Consorti was born in San Benedetto del Tronto and lives and works in Italy. He studied at Accademia di Belle Arti, Macerata. After initially working in cinema, he went on to produce work which combines painting, photography, and digital film-making. Consorti uses imagery to tell contemporary fairy stories. His imagination feeds on contemporary chronicles and personal stories, the mind's projected fantasies and anxieties. His mysterious scenes conjure up new archetypes, somewhere between a remote and primordial past and now. His first solo exhibition was at Palazzo Ducale, Urbino in 1991. Since then, he has exhibited in many countries in solo/group shows including Italy, Germany, Australia, Russia, Japan and USA.

Peter Ciccariello

Based USA

Noumena I, II, III 2009

Three photoprints

Peter Ciccariello is an interdisciplinary, cross-genre artist, poet, and photographer. His work is a pastiche of language and text in 3-D digital environments. He studied painting and design at Pratt Institute, Brooklyn, New York; Rhode Island School of Design, Providence, Rhode Island; and Parsons School of Design, New York, New York. His work has been exhibited at Harvard University, Boston, MA; The University of Arizona Poetry Center, Tucson, AZ; and at the *Interruptheque— Language driven digital art* Festival, at Brown University in Providence, USA.

Pierre-André Sonolet

Based Canada
Performance-interventions 19 and 25 July 2009
1 Bring your pigment for lunch, Vancouver
2 Bring your textile to cover up the urban infrastructure, Vancouver
Video, drawings

Originally from Paris, Pierre-André Sonolet has been based in Vancouver since 1995. Over the past two decades, his art practice has grown out of his technical training in photography, to include performance, intervention, video and installation. His works express the confrontation of human co-habiting in the built environment. His recent interests have included the intersection of the photographic and the painterly, which he explores through photographing fabric; the organic pigments that partially cover the architecture form. In parallel, he performs to investigate the 'visible and the invisible through the fabric' in the urban setting. www.pierreandresonolet.com

Richard Bartle

Based UK

Powwow 2009

Video, 6mins

Richard Bartle's work is inspired by found objects, images and texts. It is concerned with the social, the environmental, and the political and what he sees as the delicate relationship between these phenomena. The work itself has a sense of the hyper-real, it is mostly installation, often quite 'painterly', or object based, and engages with concepts of the traditional and the object in contemporary art. He has exhibited widely across the UK, and Europe, and recently attended the Platform Garanti artists' residency programme in Istanbul.

Richard Newton

Based USA

Seek no evil, Fear no evil, Be no evil 2009

3 short videos, 1min 55, 1min 34, 1min 52

Richard Newton was born in Oakland, California and currently lives in Pasadena. He has shown artworks, films and presented live performances throughout the world. His 'one-of-a-kind' books were shown at DOCUMENTA Kassel, Germany. For the *Public Spirit Festival,* the audience found him performing behind a chained door in a downtown derelict hotel. Entitled, *Get Under the Table, Don't Look at the Window,* this performance dealt with family relationships, the nature of infinity and the threat of nuclear destruction. In *The Man Who Could Eat Glass*, Newton was locked in his hotel room, ruminating on what it means to be American and to be held hostage. www.youtube.com/NewtonArtFilm

Robert Cheatham

Based USA
Pan is dead 2009
Text

Robert Cheatham is the Executive Director of Eyedrum Art and Music Gallery in Atlanta. He is also a partner in Public Domain, Inc., a non-profit organization devoted to art, theory and community, and the senior editor of PERFORATIONS, an on-line journal devoted to issues of theory, art, writing and technology. Besides being a writer, he is an installation artist, and musician. His latest project is *FORT!/da?* www.pd.org

Roland Bergere

Based Germany
Trouglodytes 2009
Audio

Roland Bergere was born in France and is a multimedia installation artist who lives and works in Cologne, Germany. Since 1983, he has worked under the name of L.O.R.

Sndsukinspook

Based UK/France
Norwich Cathedral, Norfolk, England 2009
Audio 5mins 42secs
Urban peace, Moissac harbour, Tarn et Garonne, France 2009
Audio 3mins 59secs

Lurking in the dark spaces of acous-mania, sndsukinspook forges vibrations, sculpts the harmonies that will rattle the nerves of academia. Some people scream. Some bleed to death. Disruption is everywhere. In the safe place of the sitting room, in the near inane, in the religious amnesia, in the lull of beta sofa and tv procurantism. Economia verbalis. Hypocritia interestus. Rationalitat Maladicus. Frémir le silence. Every wall has a crack. Find the wave length. www.myspace.com/nexttime

Stephan Weitzel

Based Germany
G8-Heiligendamm 2007
Series three drawings/mixed media on paper/photoprints

Stephan Weitzel was born in Stuttgart, Germany, settled in Paris and studied drama and Franco-German studies at Sorbonne-Nouvelle. He worked as a language teacher and translator and then moved to the UK where he studied art in London and Norwich. After setting up a studio in Paris, he later worked as a radio producer, film-extra and teacher. He was director's assistant/art director of Joel Cano's *Siete días Siete noches*. He has traveled and worked in Cuba, Ireland, Austria, Germany and India (New-Delhi/Kolkata, Artist-in-Residence, French Embassy) and has exhibited in solo/group shows in many countries, making interventions in public space and producing fictional and theoretical writing. Since 2007, he has lived and worked in Berlin. www.stephanweitzel.com

Tony Adams

Based Australia
Brown paper bag project 2009
Mixed media interactive installation

Tony Adams lives and works in Melbourne where he collects materials and resources from urban beaches and streets to create a variety of object-based works or installations. He is interested in exploring the aesthetic possibilities and value of 'the discarded, the displaced and the disused' and is currently completing his thesis on waste within a contemporary art context. He is collaborating with a group of artists called *SAC* (Slow Art Collective) who are working on a large scale e-waste project TS2 opening in Melbourne on Saturday 5 September 2009. www.sac-ts2.blogspot.com/

Walt Shaw

Based UK

Tiny particles pass right through your head 2009

Electronic audio, 5mins 16secs

Walt Shaw is a musician and visual/performance artist and a founder of the BET4 collective (c 1989) of musicians, performance and visual artists. He is a percussionist/drummer, currently with the Corey Mwamba /Shaw duo and Corey's *Symbiosis Ensemble, Mahood,* a free improvisation duo with musician Graham Foster, Birmingham Improvisers' Orchestra, punk- jazz group *The Dust Collectors,* and *SCHH,* an improvisation group with Bruce Coates/Mike Hurley/Chris Hobbs. His approach to percussion is experimental and improvisational, using home-made instruments, found objects and electronics. Shaw has been involved with a wealth of cross-disciplinary projects and has performed widely in the U.K, Germany and France. He is now collaborating with *Chaos Dance Company* and continues to paint and perform integrated sound/live art pieces.

Yelena Popova/David Strang

Based UK
Black series 2009
Two photoprints
Clamour Calligraphy
(with David Strang)
Video

Yelena Popova is a Russian-born artist who lives and works in Nottingham, UK. She studied set design and technology at Moscow Art Theatre School and fine art at Central Saint Martins. She is currently completing postgraduate studies at the Royal College of Art, London. She has exhibited work in Moscow, Paris, Warsaw and London and most recently showed work at the Galerie Carolyn Heinz in Hamburg. *Clamour Calligraphy* was a collaboration with the artist David Strang who uses sound to explore time-space, surface texture and interactivity. He creates soundscapes for visual artists as well as site-specific and gallery-based installations. His installations use light, sound, video, sensors and the body to explore intricate processes between both human and machine and machine and machine. www.davidstrang.co.uk

Acknowledgements

All images contained in this catalog are used with permission from the artists. In keeping with the ethic of bricolagekitchen, Creative Commons material has been used where possible. *Pan teaching Daphnis to play pipes* Heliodorus of Rhodes (copy), Palazzo Altemps, Rome photo: Jastrow, 2006 @ Wikimedia, Creative Commons. Adam Reeder kindly allowed me to reproduce an image of his *Pan* sculpture.

Thanks

The ***Pan*-demonium** project has been supported by Loughborough University School of Art and Design and AC Institute, New York. Special thanks to Danny Bright at www.bogstandardaudio.co.uk for technical assistance with audio and video and to Alan Duncan at LUSAD with printing and photography. Of course, I am extremely grateful to all at AC Institute for all their support with the exhibition and commitment to the project. Many other people have offered support and have freely given their time and expertise to this project and I would like to thank them all here.

Gillian Whiteley www.bricolagekitchen.com
gillian@bricolagekitchen.com

Loughborough University

AC Institute [Direct Chapel]

AC's mission is to advance the understanding of art through investigation, research and education. It is a lab and forum for experimentation and critical discussion. We support and develop projects that explore a performative exchange across visual, verbal and experiential disciplines. We encourage critical writing that challenges conventional expectations of meaning and objectivity as well as the boundaries between the rational and subjective. All proceeds from this catalog are dedicated to the mission of the AC Institute.

Holly Crawford, Ph.D – Director
Sonya Hofer – Fellow
Joseph Di Ponio Ph.D – Fellow

AC Institute
547 West 27th Street
Fifth Floor
New York, NY 10001
www.artcurrents.org
info@artcurrents.org

Printed in the United States on acid free paper

ISBN: 978-0-9841309-0-0
ISBN: 0-9841309-0-x

Breinigsville, PA USA
21 August 2009
222692BV00004B/2/P

9 780984 130900